The World of Mythology:
Greek Mythology

By Jim Ollhoff

VISIT US AT
WWW.ABDOPUBLISHING.COM

Published by ABDO Publishing Company, 8000 West 78th Street, Suite 310, Edina, MN 55439. Copyright ©2011 by Abdo Consulting Group, Inc. International copyrights reserved in all countries. No part of this book may be reproduced in any form without written permission from the publisher. ABDO & Daughters™ is a trademark and logo of ABDO Publishing Company.

Printed in the United States of America, North Mankato, Minnesota.
112010
012011

 PRINTED ON RECYCLED PAPER

Editor: John Hamilton
Graphic Design: Sue Hamilton
Cover Design: Neil Klinepier
Cover Photo: Neal Jany
Interior Photos & Illustrations: Alamy-pg 28; AP Images-pgs 9 & 31; Columbia Pictures (*Jason and the Argonauts*)-pg 24; Corbis-pgs 18, 22 & 25; Getty Images-pgs 5, 6, 7, 8, 10, 11 & 21; Granger Collection-pgs 14, 19, 23, 26 & 27; iStockphoto-top/bottom border & pg 16; Jacob Jordaens *Odysseus in the Cave of Polyphemus* (courtesy of the Pushkin Museum-Moscow)-pg 29; Thinkstock-pgs 4, 13, 15 & 17.

Library of Congress Cataloging-in-Publication Data

Ollhoff, Jim, 1959-
  Greek mythology / Jim Ollhoff.
    p. cm. -- (The world of mythology)
  ISBN 978-1-61714-721-0
  1. Mythology, Greek--Juvenile literature. I. Title.
  BL782.O45 2011
  398.20938--dc22
                    2010032589

CONTENTS

THE MIGHTY MYTH

Many people think a myth is a story that isn't true. They think that if something didn't actually happen, if it's not historically accurate, then it must be a myth. But that is not a very helpful way to understand myths.

Myths are stories that are important to people. Any story that guides us, comforts us, or helps us get through the day can be called a myth. Some myths are factual and historically accurate. Other myths are not.

The word *myth* comes from the Greek word *mythos*, which means "story." A myth is a story that helps us get through life. The Greeks were experts at telling important stories to help people get through life.

People in ancient times were less concerned about whether a myth was factually accurate. They were more concerned with the deeper meaning of the myth. And myths gave plenty of deep meanings! Some myths told people how to live their lives. Other myths gave important life lessons. Other myths told of gods and goddesses.

Right: A statue of Atlas, one of the older Greek gods known as Titans, is shown holding the world on his shoulders.

Above: A bronze head of Poseidon, the mythological Greek god of the sea, and a marble head of Hera, the queen of heaven and goddess of marriage. The Parthenon, temple of Athena, goddess of wisdom and war, stands in the background.

WHERE WESTERN CIVILIZATION BEGAN

Sometime before 2000 BC, people called the Mycenaeans filtered into Greece and began building communities. Because of the area's mountains and water barriers, independent city-states sprang up.

Many historians say Greece's Classical period started about the time of the first Olympic Games in 776 BC. It was after this time that a unique culture grew. It was a culture that recognized the importance of personal freedom. Especially in the city of Athens, the Greeks practiced the idea that government is better when people are involved. The study of knowledge, art, and philosophy grew. By 200 BC, Greek thinkers such as Aristotle, Socrates, and Plato had explored science and philosophy. In about 230 BC, Eratosthenes correctly calculated that the circumference of the Earth was about 25,000 miles (40,234 km).

Greek culture was so appealing that when the nearby Roman Empire spread, much of Greek culture was absorbed by the culture of the Romans. Many Greek myths were transferred into Roman mythology. In Rome, the Greek god Zeus was called by his Roman name, Jupiter. Hera was called Juno, and Poseidon was called Neptune.

Right: Early Greek Olympians including a runner, wrestlers, and a javelin thrower.

Above: Greek thinkers Plato (left, pointing upwards) and Aristotle are shown in a painting by Raphael Sanzio called *The School of Athens.*

THE SOUL OF GREECE

In ancient Greece, myths sprang up and mixed with each other as time went by. Stories that disagreed with each other existed side by side. Gods and goddesses were shared and reused in many stories. There are even different versions, with different details, of the very same myths. This situation is not unique to Greece. It occurs in the mythology of many world cultures.

Most Greek gods were pictured in human form. Many of them had the same strengths and weaknesses as humans. They got into arguments, they fell in love, they were merciful, and they became jealous. There were gods and goddesses who represented almost every part of our world. There were gods who ruled the sky, the ocean, the Earth, and the underworld. There were also gods and goddesses who ruled over the daily activities of humans, such as sleep, love, wine, drama, medicine, sports, and music. Greek mythology had less interest in the afterlife than most other cultures. Greek myths helped people with their day-to-day lives, instead of wondering about the afterlife.

Right: Dionysus, the Greek god of wine and merriment, watches a server and a dancer.

Above: An ancient Greek musician plays the lyre for a priest and a Greek king. Gods and goddesses represented almost every part of the human world.

According to the Greeks, the gods lived on Mount Olympus. This is an actual mountain in northern Greece. It is the tallest mountain in the country, and its summit is often covered in clouds. To the ancient Greeks, it was a mysterious place.

Many ancient Greek philosophers understood the deeper meanings of myths. The poet Xenophanes understood that people tried to make gods who were similar to themselves. Theagenes said that the mythological gods were symbols of human qualities. Plato said that myths were a way to communicate an important truth. In literature, this is called an allegory.

Today, Greek myths still live among us. We borrow many words and concepts from Greek myths. The names of most of the planets are the Roman names for the Greek gods. Many constellations are named after Greek myths, such as Pegasus, Orion, and the Pleiades. Our athletes compete in the Olympic Games, which got their start in ancient Greece. We talk about opening Pandora's box. We use words like discipline (from the Roman deity Disciplina) and chronology (from the Greek god Cronos). Words like fate, chlorophyll, narcissism, ocean, lunar, hygiene, liberty, and many others are borrowed from Greek mythology.

Right: According to Greek mythology, Pandora was the first woman. She was given charm and deceit by the gods. Pandora carried a box, or jar, which she opened, releasing all evils on the world.

Above: Today, athletes from around the world compete in the Olympic Games.

THE FIRST GODS

The most famous Olympic gods, including Zeus, Hera, Apollo, Hermes, and others, weren't the first gods. They were actually the grandchildren of the first gods.

According to Greek mythology, the world began when five deities, or gods, emerged from the chaos of nothing. They included Gaia (the Earth), Tartarus (the underworld), Erebus (the darkness that fills the underworld), Eros (love), and Nyx (the darkness that covers the Earth after sundown).

Nyx and Erebus had children with names like Doom, Death, Deceit, and Misery. Gaia and Uranus (the sky) also had some children. The first group of children were monsters, and the second group were Titans. The Titans were gods and goddesses who ruled for a long time. One of the leaders of the Titans was Cronos, who married Rhea. They had a number of children, including Zeus, Poseidon, and Hades.

When Zeus and his siblings grew up, they overthrew the Titans and became sole rulers of the world. They were called the Olympians.

Left: Rhea and Cronos, two of the Titan gods who had a number of children, including Zeus, Poseidon, and Hades.

Above: Zeus was the child of the Titan gods Cronos and Rhea. When Zeus and his brothers and sisters grew up, they overthrew the Titans and became the Olympic gods.

THE OLYMPIC GODS

Many ancient manuscripts refer to the 12 gods who lived on Mount Olympus. But the list of exactly which gods lived on Mount Olympus differs between writers.

Zeus is included on all of the lists of the Olympic gods. He was the sky god, the most powerful deity in Greek mythology. He threw thunderbolts when he was angry. His Roman name was Jupiter.

Hera was the sister and wife of Zeus, and the queen of Mount Olympus. She was the goddess of marriage and motherhood. The stories often reveal her to be hateful and full of spite. Her Roman name was Juno.

Poseidon was the god of the sea. He was the second-most powerful god, after his brother Zeus. When Poseidon became angry, he caused earthquakes. Often pictured with a trident, his Roman name was Neptune.

Above: Hera, queen of Olympus, pictured in a chariot being pulled by peacocks.

Above: Poseidon, the Greek god of the sea, is often pictured with his trident.

Aphrodite was the goddess of love and beauty. Her Roman name was Venus. One of the most famous statues in the world, the Venus de Milo, is believed to be of the goddess Aphrodite. All that is left is the torso and head of the Venus de Milo. Her arms were broken off sometime in the past. The statue today is in the Louvre Museum in Paris, France.

Apollo was the god of music, poetry, and healing. He is often pictured with a bow and arrow, or a lyre, a harp-like stringed instrument.

Other Olympic gods included Hades, the god of the underworld, where dead people reside. His Roman name was Pluto. Hermes (Roman name: Mercury) was the messenger god. He played lots of tricks on people and other gods. He is usually pictured wearing a winged hat and winged sandals to show his speed. Ares (Roman name: Mars) was the god of war. Hephaestus (Roman name: Vulcan) was the god of fire and blacksmithing. Dionysus (Roman name: Bacchus) was the god of wine. Olympic goddesses included Hestia (Roman name: Vesta), the goddess of the hearth, or the fireplace in the home. Demeter (Roman name: Ceres) was the goddess of the harvest. The goddess of the hunt was Artemis (Roman name: Diana), and the goddess of wisdom was Athena (Roman name: Minerva).

Left: Hermes was the messenger god. He wears a winged hat and sandals to show his speed, and holds a special staff called a caduceus.

Above: Aphrodite was the goddess of love and beauty.

THE CREATION OF PEOPLE

Two Titan brothers, Prometheus and Epimetheus, had the task of creating all the creatures in the world. Prometheus was wise, but Epimetheus was not very intelligent. Epimetheus created creatures, giving each of them gifts, such as sharp teeth, claws, or wings. However, Epimetheus didn't plan ahead, and he ran out of gifts just before humans were created. Prometheus came to the rescue. He made humans to look like the gods, and then made sure they had fire to heat their homes and cook their food.

Zeus was very angry that Prometheus gave away the secret of fire.

As a punishment, Zeus chained him to a rock, and every day an eagle came and pecked out his liver. Prometheus's liver grew back every night. Day after day, the torture repeated. Later, Zeus changed his mind and asked Heracles (Roman name: Hercules) to rescue Prometheus.

Left: Prometheus takes fire from Mount Olympus to give to humans to heat their homes and cook their food.

Above: Zeus was angry that Prometheus gave people the secret of fire, so he chained the Titan to a rock. Every day an eagle pecked out Prometheus's liver. Every night, it grew back. Day after day, the torture was repeated, until Zeus finally changed his mind.

THE ORIGIN OF THE SEASONS

Demeter was the grain mother and protector-goddess of the crops. She had a daughter named Persephone. Persephone was very beautiful. Many of the gods wanted to marry her. However, Hades, the god of the underworld, kidnapped her and took her to the underworld to be his wife.

Demeter was grief-stricken. She left Mount Olympus and wandered all over the countryside, looking for her daughter. Some of the Greek myths say she was so busy looking for her daughter that she forgot to keep the crops growing. Other versions of the story say that she was so enraged that she withheld the harvest of the crops. Without crops, humanity suffered in hunger.

Zeus sent Hermes to the underworld to rescue Persephone. Unfortunately, Hades tricked Persephone into eating some pomegranate seeds. One of the rules of the underworld was that anyone who ate any kind of food had to stay there. So, Hermes rescued Persephone, but she had to return to the underworld for four months every year to be with her husband, Hades. During this time, Demeter withheld the harvest. The land froze over and nothing grew. Every spring, Persephone was reunited with her mother, and Demeter was so happy that flowers bloomed and crops grew.

Demeter's Roman name is Ceres. From this name for the goddess of grain, we get our word for cereal.

Above: Hermes rescues Persephone from the underworld and returns the girl to Demeter, her mother. However, Persephone returns to the underworld four months each year.

HERACLES

One of the most popular figures of Greek mythology is Heracles. (Today he is more often known by his Roman name, Hercules.) Heracles was a half-god. He was the son of Zeus and a mortal woman. Heracles was famous for his strength and bravery.

There are many stories of his adventures. Perhaps the most famous are his Twelve Labors. As punishment for killing his own children in a mad frenzy, Heracles was made to serve King Eurystheus of Mycenae. King Eurystheus asked Heracles to do 12 tasks.

The first task was to fight the Nemean Lion. This was a terrible monster in the shape of a lion, although some of the myths said it sometimes appeared as a beautiful woman so it could lure people to their deaths. The lion's skin was impervious, so weapons were useless against it. Heracles had to fight the monster with his bare hands. He killed it by choking it to death.

Other tasks that Heracles had to perform included killing the nine-headed hydra, capturing King Minos's bull from Crete, and bringing back the belt of Hippolyta, the feared warrior-queen of the Amazons.

Right: Heracles is shown fighting Nemean the lion. This was one of the strong, half-god's 12 tasks.

Above: An illustration of Heracles fighting the nine-headed hydra.

JASON AND THE GOLDEN FLEECE

The story of Jason and the Argonauts is one of the most famous and best-loved stories in Western civilization. Jason was the rightful heir to be king, but his uncle, Pelias, took the throne instead. Jason wanted the kingship back. Pelias said that he would give the throne to Jason if he accomplished a heroic task. He challenged Jason to find and bring back the Golden Fleece, the legendary pelt of a flying ram made of gold. The quest to find the fleece would require a long sea journey, and there would be many obstacles and much danger along the way. Jason's uncle was sure that it was an impossible task.

Jason assembled a crew of great heroes who would sail with him on his ship, the *Argo*. The adventurers were known as the Argonauts. They would sail to a land called Colchis to get the Golden Fleece. They sailed past the place where Prometheus was chained to a rock. They sailed through a dangerous place called the Symplegades, where two giant rocks smashed together and crushed anything passing through. Jason released a dove through the rocks, and then the rocks shut. Jason timed the opening of the rocks and got through before they could close again. The Argonauts also had to battle the Harpies, bird-women who caught and tortured people.

A Harpie.

Above: Jason and the Argonauts on their voyage to bring back the Golden Fleece.

Jason finally arrived in the land of Colchis and asked King Aeëtes to give him the Golden Fleece. The King disliked Jason and gave him a dangerous task. In order to get the fleece, Jason first had to plow a field using fire-breathing bulls. Next, he had to plant the soil with dragon teeth, which would instantly sprout an army of armed warriors.

Luckily, the goddess Hera was on Jason's side. She made the king's daughter, Medea, fall in love with Jason. Medea was a sorceress, and she used her magic to help Jason defeat the dragon-tooth army.

Jason finally found the Golden Fleece, but it was guarded by a dragon. Medea's magic put the creature to sleep. Jason grabbed the fleece, escaped to his ship, and then he and the Argonauts sailed back to Greece.

Right: Jason waves to Medea as he plows a field using fire-breathing bulls.

Above: After many dangerous tasks, Jason finally found the Golden Fleece. He and his men sailed with it back to Greece.

THE VOYAGES OF ODYSSEUS

Another favorite Greek myth is the story of Odysseus (Roman name: Ulysses). After the Trojan War was over, Odysseus was on his way home, but his ships were blown off course. He had many adventures while trying to get home.

On one stop, Odysseus had to battle a Cyclops. The Cyclops was a huge giant with only one eye in the center of its forehead. Odysseus and his crew were trapped in the Cyclops's cave, and the Cyclops was eating Odysseus's crew. Odysseus told the Cyclops his name was "Nobody," then tricked him into drinking too much wine.

The Cyclops in front of his cave.

When the Cyclops fell down from drinking too much, Odysseus plunged a stake into the giant's eye. The Cyclops started screaming, causing another Cyclops to shout into the cave and ask what was wrong. The blind Cyclops shouted, "Nobody is hurting me!" The other Cyclopses, thinking that everything was okay, went home. Odysseus and each of his crew escaped the cave by hanging onto the wool underneath the sheep. The blind monster groped the sheep, but didn't notice the men clinging underneath.

Odysseus and his men escape from the blind Cyclops.

GLOSSARY

AMAZONS

A legendary tribe of all-female warriors.

CYCLOPS

A giant monster with one eye in the center of its forehead.

DIETIES

Another name for gods and goddesses in ancient Greece.

HYDRA

From Greek mythology, a snake or dragon with multiple (usually seven or nine) heads. If one head was cut off, two more grew back in its place. The head in the middle was immortal, and could not be killed.

IMPERVIOUS

Not allowing a substance or object to pass through. For example, when Heracles tried to fight Nemean the lion, the hero discovered that his weapons could not pass through the lion's skin.

MOUNT OLYMPUS

The mountain where the Greek gods lived.

MYCENAEANS

The people who likely settled in Greece before 2000 BC.

MYTHOS

A Greek word that means "story."

PHILOSOPHY

The study of knowledge and beliefs. A way of looking at the world and our place in it.

TRIDENT

A three-pronged spear, often used in fishing. Poseidon, god of the sea, is often shown holding a trident.

TROJAN WAR

A war fought by the Greeks against the city of Troy.

UNDERWORLD

A place under the Earth where the dead reside.

VENUS DE MILO

A statue believed to be of Aphrodite (Roman name: Venus). The statue is in the Louvre Museum in Paris, France.

Venus de Milo

INDEX